BASIC SET #2

RUDIMENTS EXAM SERIES ANSWERS

By Glory St. Germain ARCT RMT MYCC UMTC &
Shelagh McKibbon-U'Ren RMT UMTC

GSG MUSIC

Enriching Lives Through Music Education

ISBN: 978-1-927641-11-8

# The Ultimate Music Theory™ Program

Enriching Lives Through Music Education

The Ultimate Music Theory™ Workbooks & Answer Books Program includes:

UMT Rudiments Workbooks for Prep 1, Prep 2, Basic, Intermediate, Advanced & Complete
UMT Exam Series (Set #1 & Set #2) for Preparatory, Basic, Intermediate & Advanced

Supplemental Workbooks for PREP LEVEL, LEVELS 1 - 8 & COMPLETE LEVEL
UMT Supplemental Exam Series for LEVEL 5, LEVEL 6, LEVEL 7 & LEVEL 8

The Ultimate Music Theory Program is the *Way to Score Success* as UMT helps students prepare for nationally recognized theory examinations including the Royal Conservatory of Music.

 Library and Archives Canada Cataloguing in Publication. UMT Workbooks & Exam Series /Glory St. Germain & Shelagh McKibbon-U'Ren. Respect Copyright. All rights reserved. GlorylandPublishing.com

Ultimate Music Theory Rudiments Exam Series

GP - EPS1	ISBN: 978-1-927641-00-2	Preparatory Rudiments Exams Set #1
GP - EPS1A	ISBN: 978-1-927641-08-8	Preparatory Exams Answers Set #1
GP - EPS2	ISBN: 978-1-927641-01-9	Preparatory Rudiments Exams Set #2
GP - EPS2A	ISBN: 978-1-927641-09-5	Preparatory Exams Answers Set #2
GP - EBS1	ISBN: 978-1-927641-02-6	Basic Rudiments Exams Set #1
GP - EBS1A	ISBN: 978-1-927641-10-1	Basic Exams Answers Set #1
GP - EBS2	ISBN: 978-1-927641-03-3	Basic Rudiments Exams Set #2
GP - EBS2A	ISBN: 978-1-927641-11-8	Basic Exams Answers Set #2
GP - EIS1	ISBN: 978-1-927641-04-0	Intermediate Rudiments Exams Set #1
GP - EIS1A	ISBN: 978-1-927641-12-5	Intermediate Exams Answers Set #1
GP - EIS2	ISBN: 978-1-927641-05-7	Intermediate Rudiments Exams Set #2
GP - EIS2A	ISBN: 978-1-927641-13-2	Intermediate Exams Answers Set #2
GP - EAS1	ISBN: 978-1-927641-06-4	Advanced Rudiments Exams Set #1
GP - EAS1A	ISBN: 978-1-927641-14-9	Advanced Exams Answers Set #1
GP - EAS2	ISBN: 978-1-927641-07-1	Advanced Rudiments Exams Set #2
GP - EAS2A	ISBN: 978-1-927641-15-6	Advanced Exams Answers Set #2

Ultimate Music Theory Supplemental Exam Series

GP-L5E	ISBN: 978-1-990358-11-1	LEVEL 5 Exams
GP-L5EA	ISBN: 978-1-990358-12-8	LEVEL 5 Exams Answers
GP-L6E	ISBN: 978-1-990358-13-5	LEVEL 6 Exams
GP-L6EA	ISBN: 978-1-990358-14-2	LEVEL 6 Exams Answers
GP-L7E	ISBN: 978-1-990358-15-9	LEVEL 7 Exams
GP-L7EA	ISBN: 978-1-990358-16-6	LEVEL 7 Exams Answers
GP-L8E	ISBN: 978-1-990358-17-3	LEVEL 8 Exams
GP-L8EA	ISBN: 978-1-990358-18-0	LEVEL 8 Exams Answers

Go to UltimateMusicTheory.com and check out the FREE Resources

Ultimate Music Theory FREE RESOURCES created just for you!

The **Ultimate Music Theory Exams** reinforce the **UMT Basic Rudiments Workbook** and prepare students for continued learning with UMT Intermediate Rudiments.

Basic Rudiments Theory Examination requirements are:

Pitch
- Grand Staff (Treble Clef or G Clef and Bass Clef or F Clef)
- Note names (up to five ledger lines below and above the Treble Clef and Bass Clef)
- Accidentals (sharp, flat and natural signs)
- Whole tones (whole steps), diatonic & chromatic semitones (half steps) and enharmonic equivalents

Rhythm
- Note and rest time values (whole, half, quarter, eighth and sixteenth)
- Dotted half notes, dotted quarter notes and dotted eighth notes
- Triplets (quarter notes, eighth notes and sixteenth notes)
- Adding Time Signatures, bar lines and rests to a given line of music (which may include an anacrusis)
- Simple Time Signatures ($\frac{2}{2}$, ¢, $\frac{3}{2}$, $\frac{4}{2}$, $\frac{2}{4}$, $\frac{3}{4}$, $\frac{4}{4}$, C, $\frac{2}{8}$, $\frac{3}{8}$ and $\frac{4}{8}$)

Scales in Major and minor keys up to and including four sharps and four flats
- Major and relative minor (natural, harmonic and melodic) scales, ascending and descending
- Key Signatures (Major and relative minor)
- Tonic, Subdominant and Dominant scale degrees

Triads in Major and harmonic minor keys up to and including four sharps and four flats
- Write or identify: Solid triads (blocked) in Root Position (close position only) beginning on the Tonic, Subdominant and Dominant notes (with or without a Key Signature)
- Identify: Broken triads in Root Position (close position only) beginning on the Tonic, Subdominant and Dominant notes (with or without a Key Signature)

Intervals - Perfect, Major and minor
- Write or identify: above a given note, all intervals up to and including an octave (no inversions), melodic or harmonic form (with or without a Key Signature)
- Identify: below a given note, all intervals up to and including an octave (no inversions), melodic form only (with or without a Key Signature)

Recognition of Key Signatures up to and including four sharps and four flats
- Identify the key (Major or minor) of a given melody with a Key Signature

Transposition (keys up to and including four sharps and four flats)
- Transpose a melody up or down one octave
- Transpose a melody from one clef to another (Treble to Bass or Bass to Treble)
- Rewrite a melody at the same pitch in the alternate clef

Musical Terms and Signs
- Recognize, define or give the musical terms or signs as listed in the Basic Rudiments Workbook

Analysis
- Analyze a short musical composition, identifying any of the above theory requirements

Score:
  60 - 69 Pass; 70 - 79 Honors; 80 - 89 First Class Honors; 90 - 100 First Class Honors with Distinction

Ultimate Music Theory: *The Way to Score Success!*

UltimateMusicTheory.com © Copyright 2013 Gloryland Publishing. All Rights Reserved.

ULTIMATE MUSIC THEORY
BASIC EXAM SET #2 - EXAM #1

Total Score: ___ / 100

1. a) Write the following notes on ledger lines either above or below the Treble Clef. Use half notes.

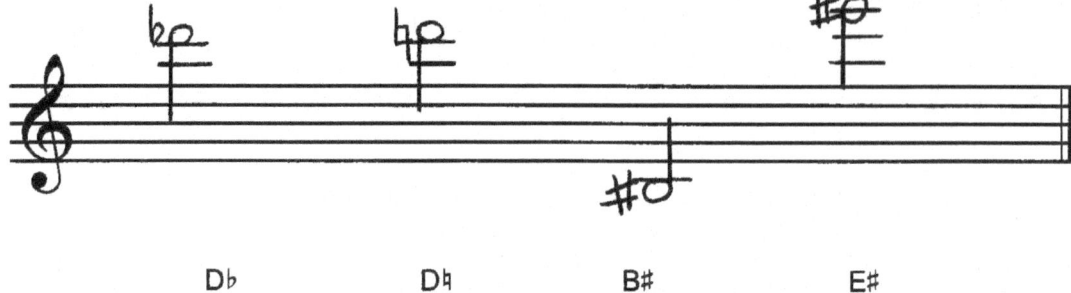

        Db   Dh   B#   E#

b) In the measure beside each note, write its enharmonic equivalent. Use whole notes. Name both notes.

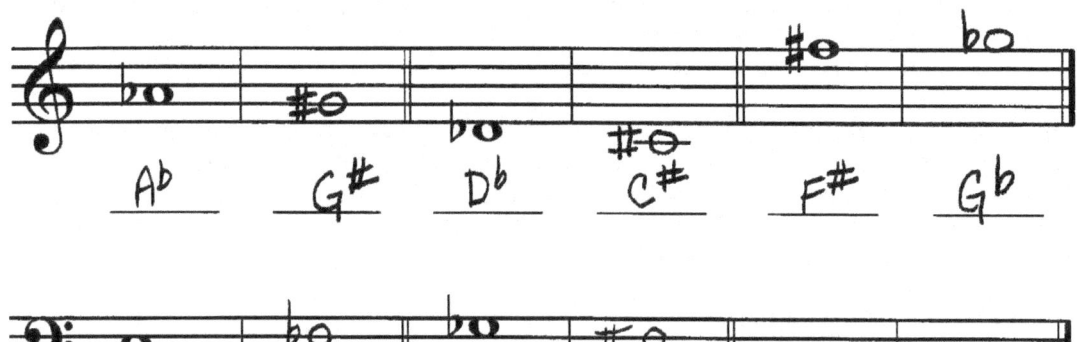

Ab G#   Db C#   F# Gb

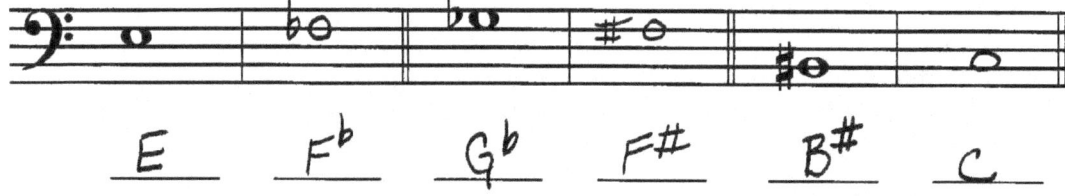

E Fb   Gb F#   B# C

c) Name the note below each bracket.

F# A   C# A

UltimateMusicTheory.com © Copyright 2013 Gloryland Publishing. All Rights Reserved.

ULTIMATE MUSIC THEORY
BASIC EXAM SET #2 - EXAM #1

2. a) Write the following solid triads in root position in the Bass Clef. Use accidentals. Use whole notes.

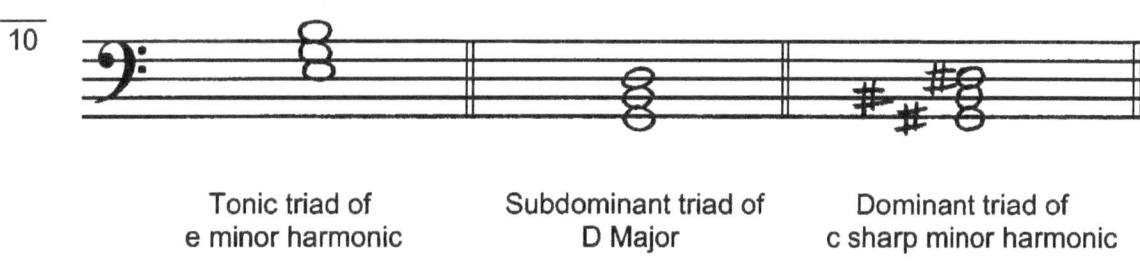

Tonic triad of e minor harmonic   Subdominant triad of D Major   Dominant triad of c sharp minor harmonic

b) Match each description in the left column with the correct triad in the right column.

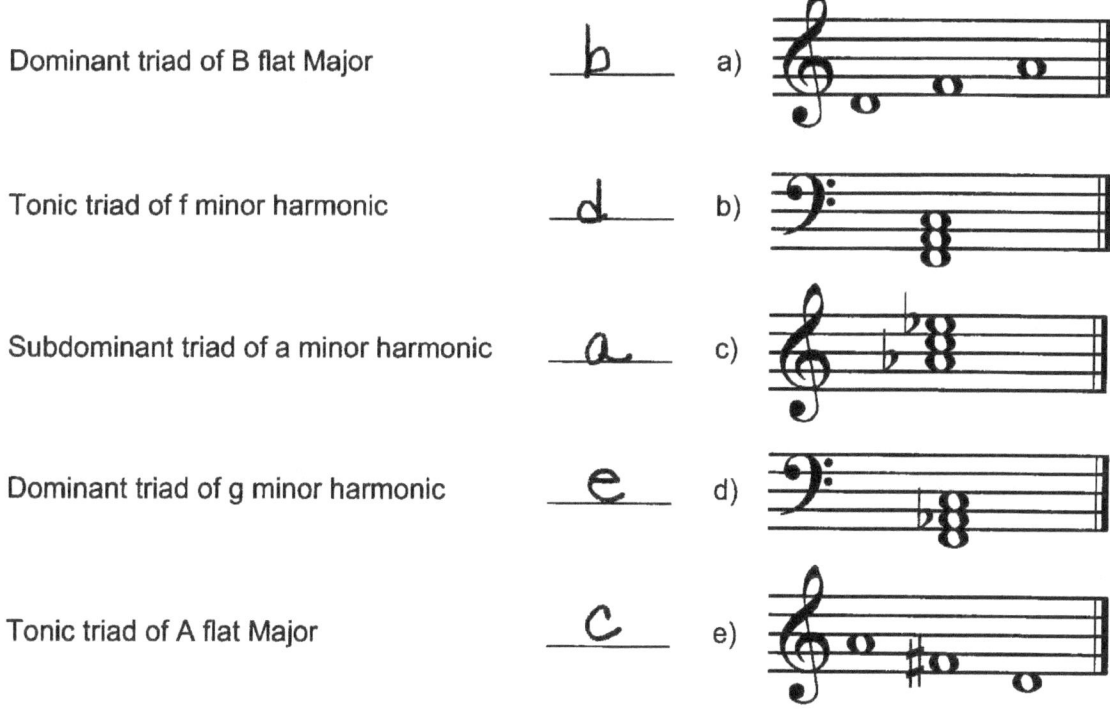

Dominant triad of B flat Major   _b_

Tonic triad of f minor harmonic   _d_

Subdominant triad of a minor harmonic   _a_

Dominant triad of g minor harmonic   _e_

Tonic triad of A flat Major   _c_

c) Name the following notes.

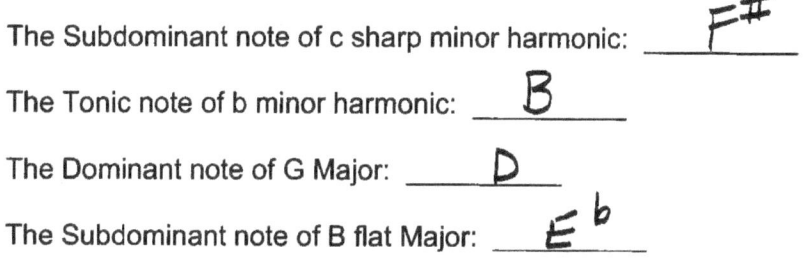

The Subdominant note of c sharp minor harmonic: __F#__

The Tonic note of b minor harmonic: __B__

The Dominant note of G Major: __D__

The Subdominant note of B flat Major: __Eb__

ULTIMATE MUSIC THEORY
BASIC EXAM SET #2 - EXAM #1

3. a) Name the following intervals.

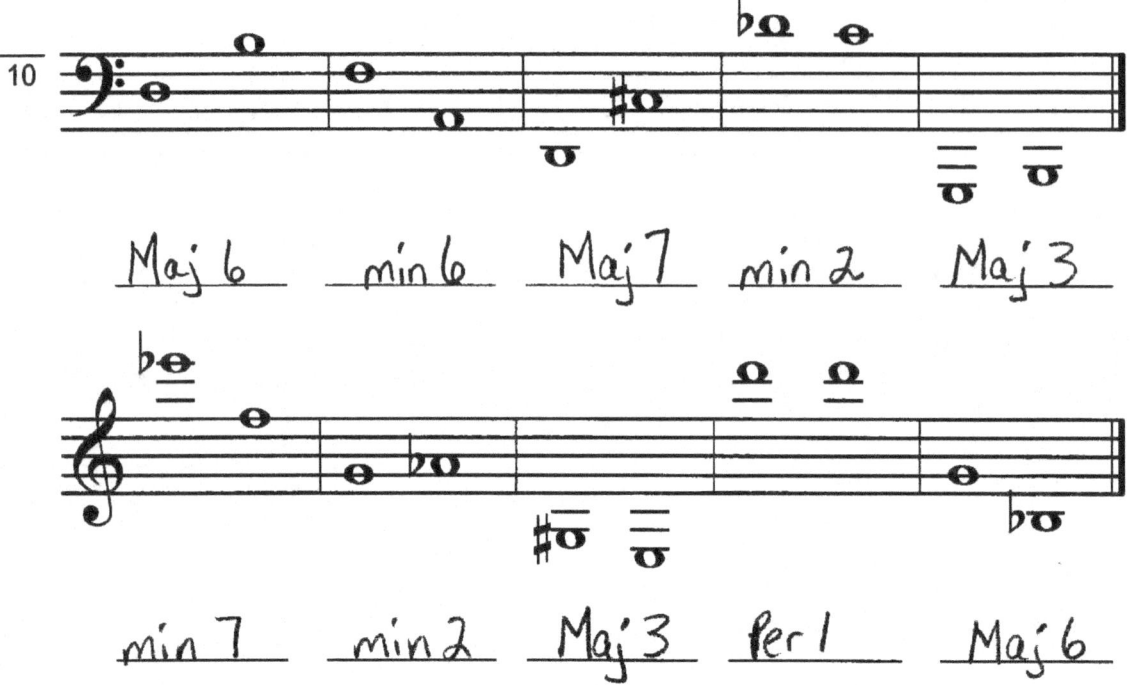

b) Write the melodic interval above each of the given notes. Use half notes.

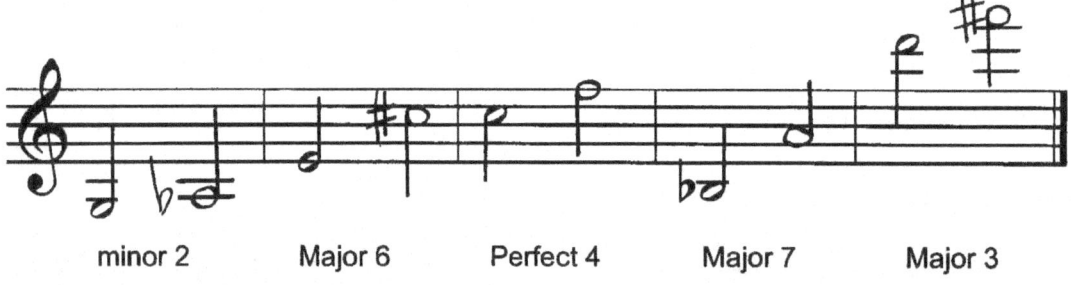

c) Write the harmonic interval above each of the given notes. Use whole notes.

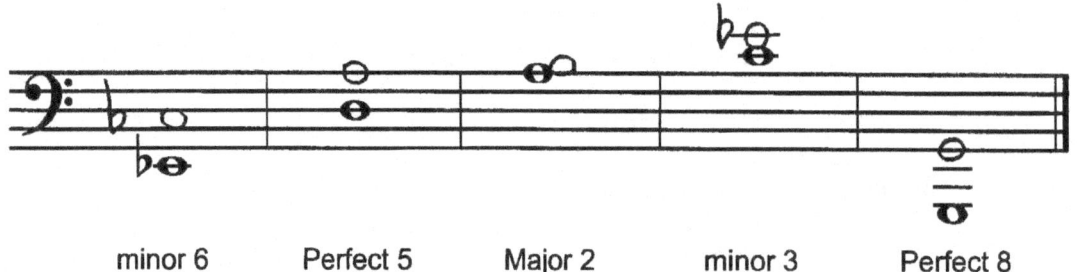

ULTIMATE MUSIC THEORY
BASIC EXAM SET #2 - EXAM #1

4. a) Name the key of the following melody. Rewrite the melody at the same pitch in the Treble Clef.

Key: B♭ Major

b) Name the key of the following melody. Transpose it down one octave in the Bass Clef.

Key: C# minor

ULTIMATE MUSIC THEORY
BASIC EXAM SET #2 - EXAM #1

5. a) Name each of the following scales and specify its type (Major, natural minor, harmonic minor or melodic minor).

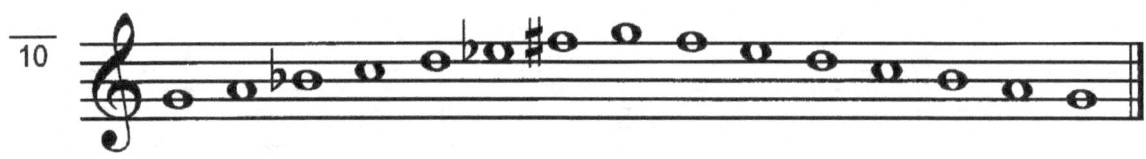

Scale: g minor harmonic

Scale: A♭ Major

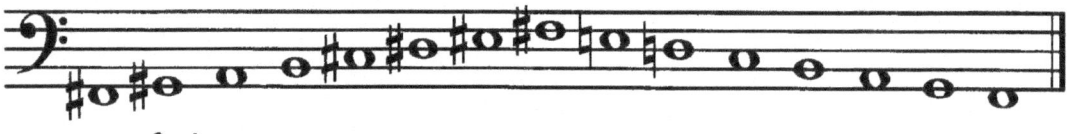

Scale: f# minor melodic

b) Write the b minor natural scale, ascending and descending, in the Treble Clef. Use accidentals. Use whole notes.

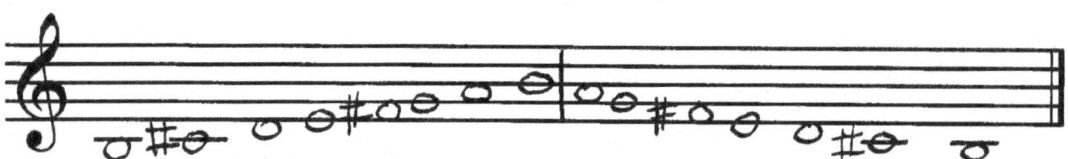

c) Write the F Major scale, ascending and descending, in the Bass Clef. Use a Key Signature. Use whole notes.

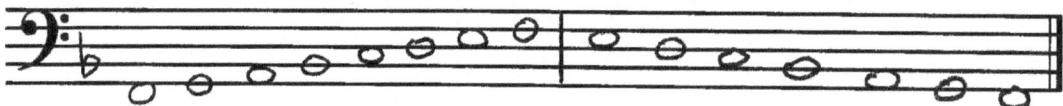

UltimateMusicTheory.com © Copyright 2013 Gloryland Publishing. All Rights Reserved.

ULTIMATE MUSIC THEORY
BASIC EXAM SET #2 - EXAM #1

6. a) Name the Major key for each of the following Key Signatures.
    b) Name each of the given notes as: Tonic (**T**)
                                         Subdominant (**SD**)
                                         or Dominant (**D**)

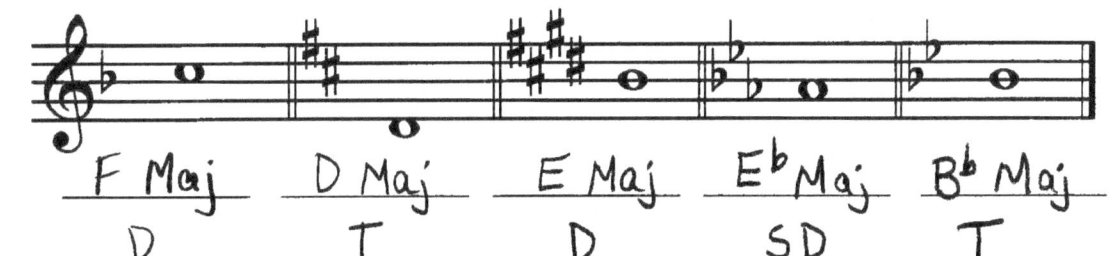

a) F Maj | D Maj | E Maj | E♭ Maj | B♭ Maj
b) D | T | D | SD | T

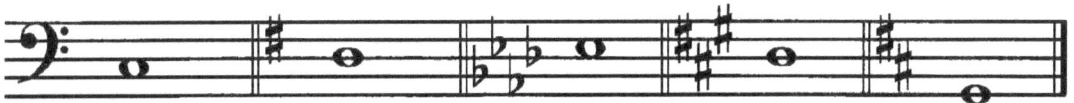

a) C Maj | G Maj | A♭ Maj | A Maj | D Maj
b) T | D | D | SD | SD

c) Name each of the following as: diatonic semitone or diatonic half step (**d.s.**)
                                   chromatic semitone or chromatic half step (**c.s.**)
                                   whole tone or whole step (**w.t.**)
                                   or enharmonic equivalent (**e.e.**)

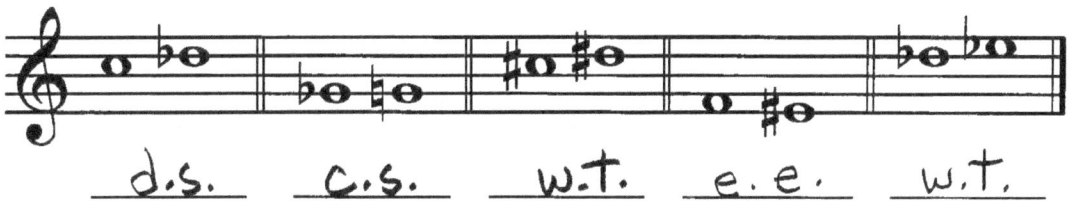

d.s. | c.s. | w.t. | e.e. | w.t.

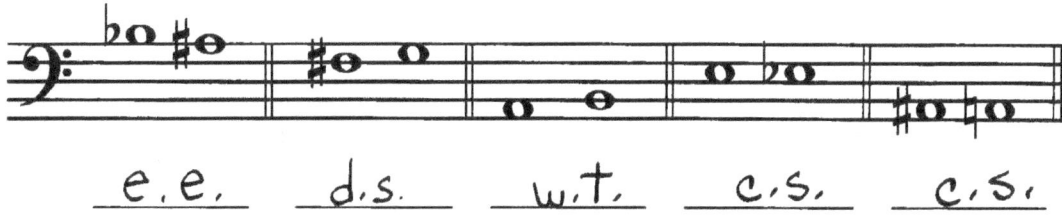

e.e. | d.s. | w.t. | c.s. | c.s.

ULTIMATE MUSIC THEORY
BASIC EXAM SET #2 - EXAM #1

7. a) Add bar lines to complete each of the following rhythms.

b) Add the correct Time Signature under each bracket to complete the following rhythms.

ULTIMATE MUSIC THEORY
BASIC EXAM SET #2 - EXAM #1

8. Add rests below each bracket to complete each measure.

ULTIMATE MUSIC THEORY
BASIC EXAM SET #2 - EXAM #1

9. Match each musical term with its English definition. (Not all definitions will be used.)

	Term		Definition
10			
			a) slow
	prestissimo	f	b) detached
	Tempo primo (Tempo I)	j	c) moderately soft
	lento	a	d) not as slow as largo
	fine	h	e) majestic
	legato	k	f) as fast as possible
	maestoso	e	g) moderately slow; at a walking pace
	staccato	b	h) the end
	larghetto	d	i) graceful
	cantabile	l	j) return to the original tempo
	andante	g	k) smooth
			l) in a singing style

UltimateMusicTheory.com © Copyright 2013 Gloryland Publishing. All Rights Reserved.

ULTIMATE MUSIC THEORY
BASIC EXAM SET #2 - EXAM #1

10. Analyze the following piece of music by answering the questions below.

Pitter Patter

Prestissimo   S. McKibbon

[Musical score with labeled sections A, B, C, D, E, F, G]

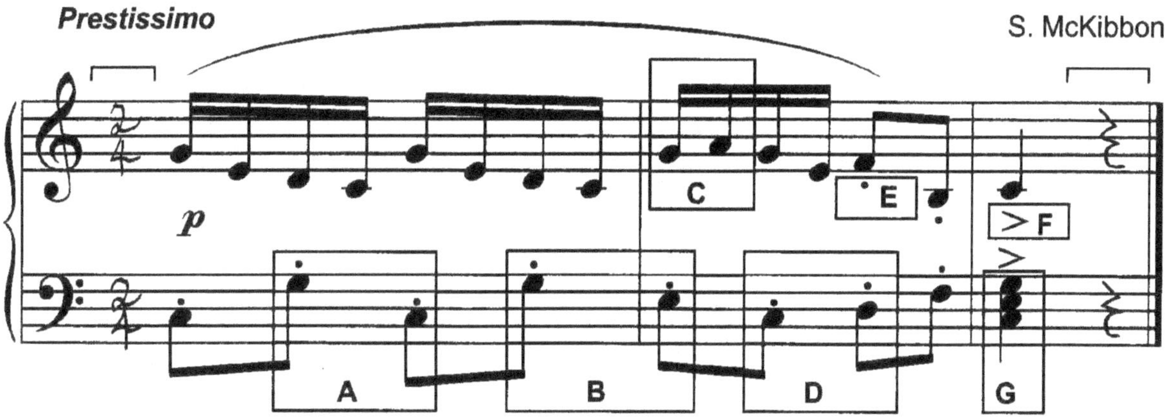

a) Name the title of this piece. **Pitter Patter**

b) Explain the tempo of this piece. **as fast as possible**

c) Add the Time Signature directly on the music.

d) Name the key of this piece. **C Major**

e) Name the intervals at the letters: A **Per 5**   B **min 3**

f) Name the intervals at the letters: C **Maj 2**   D **Maj 2**

g) Explain the sign at the letter E. **staccato - detached**

h) Explain the sign at the letter F. **accent - stressed note**

i) Is the triad at the letter G Major or minor? **Major**

j) In measure three, add the missing rest in the Treble Clef and in the Bass Clef.

ULTIMATE MUSIC THEORY
BASIC EXAM SET #2 - EXAM #2

Total Score: ___/100

1. a) Write the following notes on ledger lines either above or below the Treble Clef. Use quarter notes.

/10

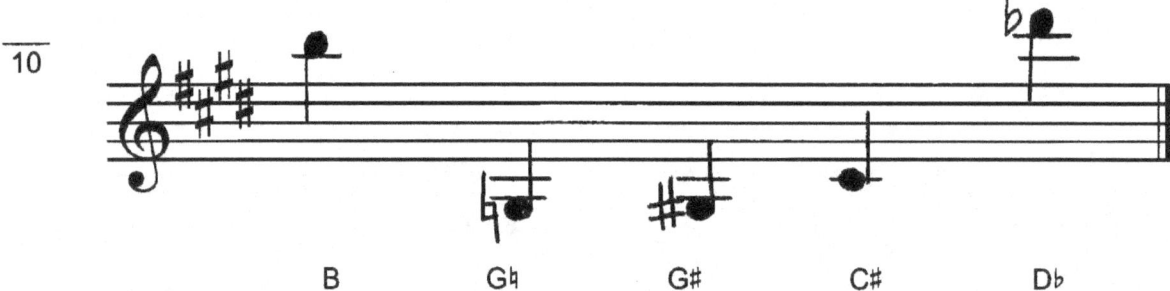

      B   G♮   G♯   C♯   D♭

b) Name the note below each bracket.

    F   A   E   G   F

c) Write the following notes in the Bass Clef. Do not use ledger lines. Use half notes.

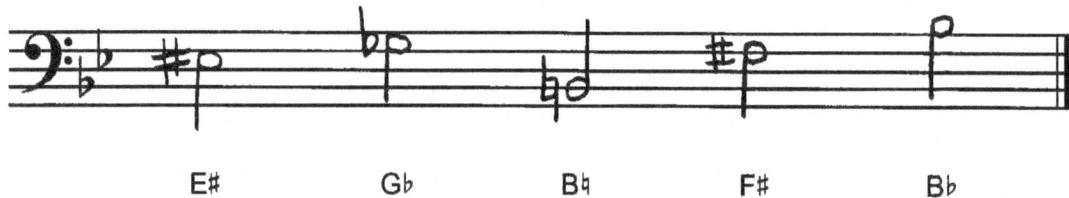

  E♯   G♭   B♮   F♯   B♭

d) Name the note below each bracket.

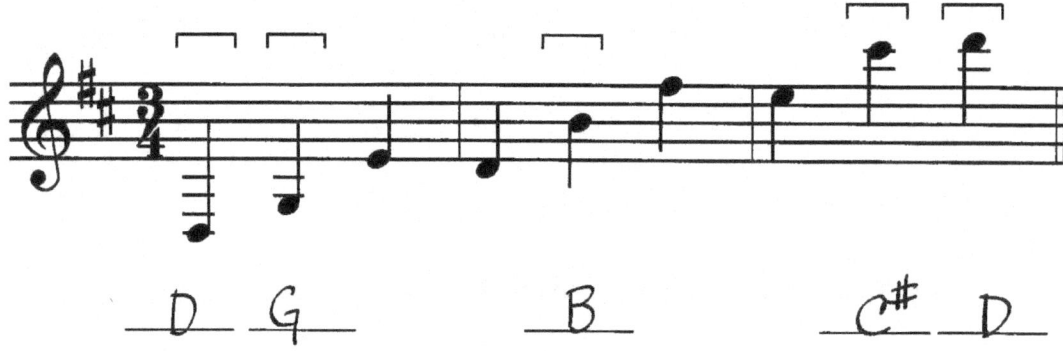

  D G   B   C♯ D

ULTIMATE MUSIC THEORY
BASIC EXAM SET #2 - EXAM #2

2. a) Write the following notes in the Bass Clef. Use a Key Signature and any necessary accidentals. Use whole notes.

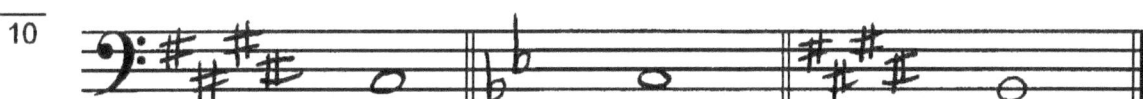

| Tonic note of | Subdominant note of | Dominant note of |
| c sharp minor harmonic | g minor harmonic | E Major |

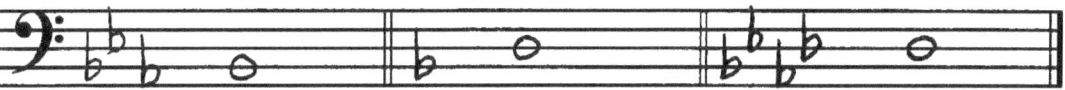

| Dominant note of | Tonic note of | Subdominant note of |
| E flat Major | d minor harmonic | A flat Major |

b) Write the following solid (blocked) triads in root position in the Treble Clef. Use accidentals. Use whole notes.

Tonic triad of
f sharp minor harmonic

Dominant triad of
b minor harmonic

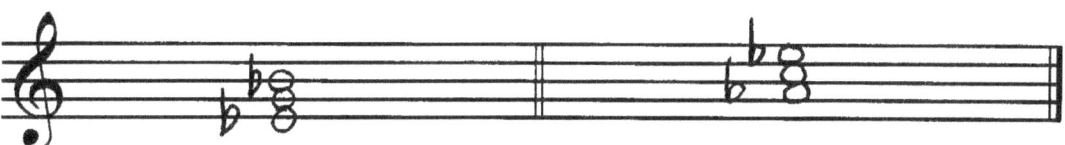

Dominant triad of
A flat Major

Subdominant triad of
E flat Major

ULTIMATE MUSIC THEORY
BASIC EXAM SET #2 - EXAM #2

3. a) Name the following intervals.

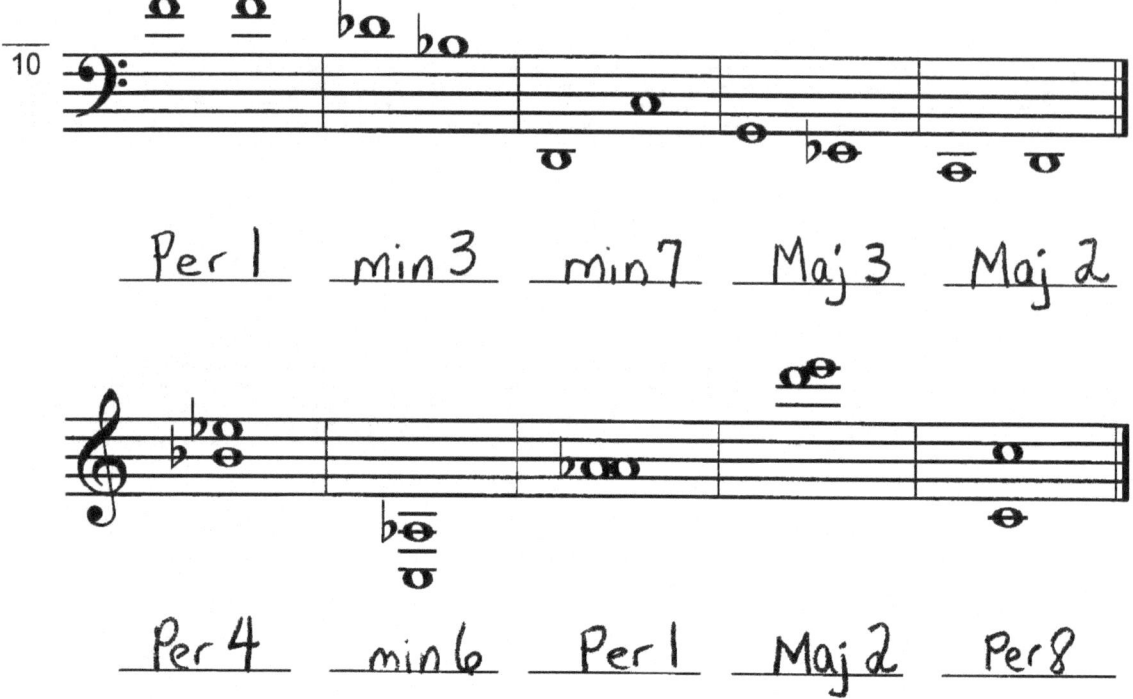

b) Write the melodic interval above each of the given notes. Use half notes.

Perfect 1   minor 7   Major 6   Perfect 4   minor 2

c) Write the harmonic interval above each of the given notes. Use whole notes.

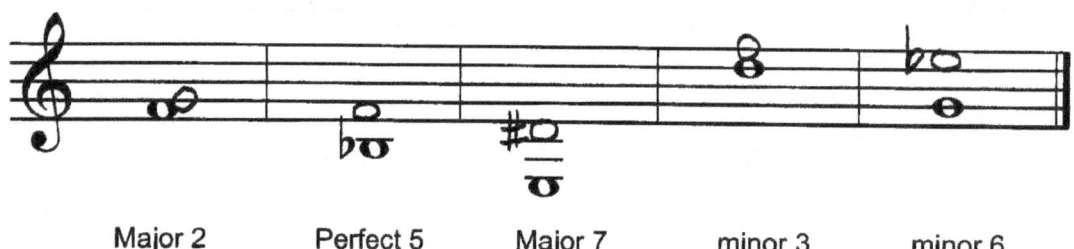

Major 2   Perfect 5   Major 7   minor 3   minor 6

UltimateMusicTheory.com © Copyright 2013 Gloryland Publishing. All Rights Reserved.

ULTIMATE MUSIC THEORY
BASIC EXAM SET #2 - EXAM #2

4. a) Name the key of the following melody. Transpose it down one octave in the Bass Clef.

Key: __C Major__

b) Name the key of the following melody. Transpose it up one octave in the Treble Clef.

Key: __f minor__

ULTIMATE MUSIC THEORY
BASIC EXAM SET #2 - EXAM #2

5. a) Write the a minor harmonic scale, ascending and descending, in the Bass Clef.
   Use accidentals. Use whole notes.

b) Write the E flat Major scale, ascending and descending, in the Treble Clef.
   Use accidentals. Use whole notes.

c) Write the c sharp minor natural scale, ascending and descending, in the Bass Clef.
   Use accidentals. Use whole notes.

d) Write the E Major scale, ascending and descending, in the Treble Clef.
   Use a Key Signature. Use whole notes.

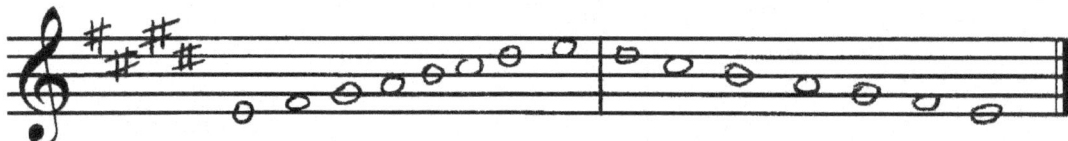

e) Identify the minor key for the following Key Signatures.

_f#_ minor   _e_ minor   _d_ minor   _f_ minor

UltimateMusicTheory.com © Copyright 2013 Gloryland Publishing. All Rights Reserved.

ULTIMATE MUSIC THEORY
BASIC EXAM SET #2 - EXAM #2

6. a) Name the minor key for each of the following Key Signatures.
   b) Name each of the given notes as: Tonic (**T**)
      Subdominant (**SD**)
      or Dominant (**D**)

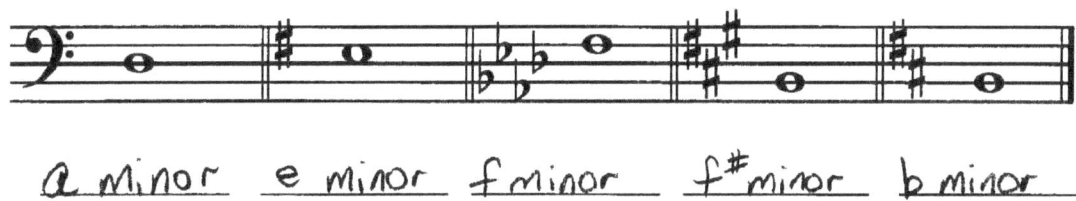

a) a minor   e minor   f minor   f# minor   b minor
b)   SD   T   T   SD   T

a) d minor   g minor   c minor   c# minor   f minor
b)   T   SD   D   D   SD

c) Name each of the following as: diatonic semitone or diatonic half step (**d.s.**)
   chromatic semitone or chromatic half step (**c.s.**)
   whole tone or whole step (**w.t.**)
   or enharmonic equivalent (**e.e.**)

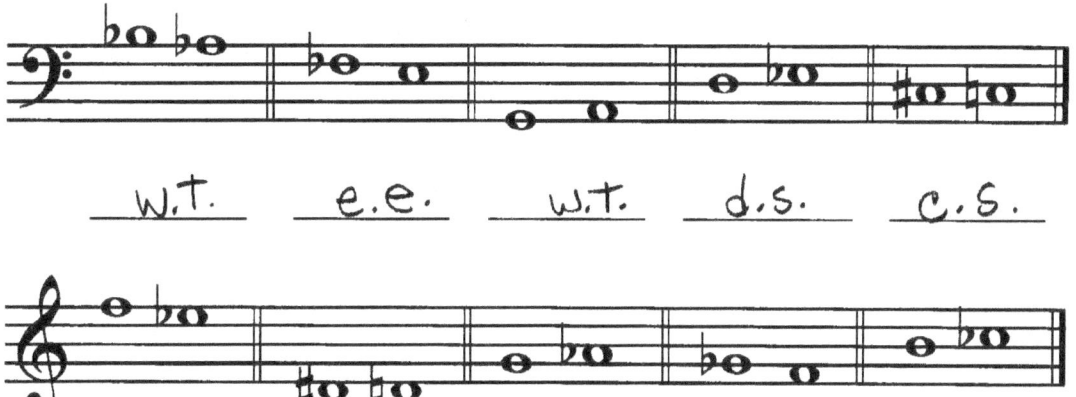

   w.t.   e.e.   w.t.   d.s.   c.s.

   w.t.   c.s.   d.s.   d.s.   e.e.

ULTIMATE MUSIC THEORY
BASIC EXAM SET #2 - EXAM #2

7. a) Add the correct Time Signature under each bracket to complete the following rhythms.

b) Add bar lines to complete each of the following rhythms.

ULTIMATE MUSIC THEORY
BASIC EXAM SET #2 - EXAM #2

8. Add rests below each bracket to complete each measure.

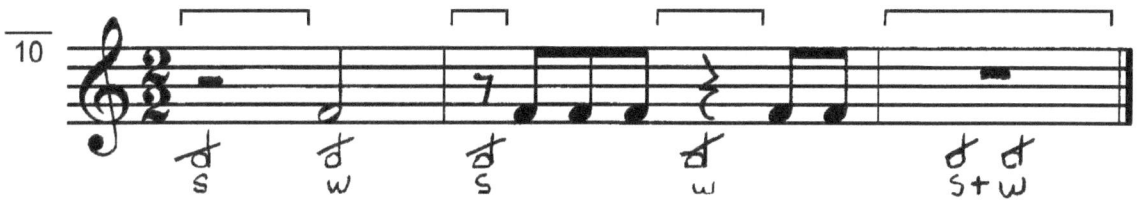

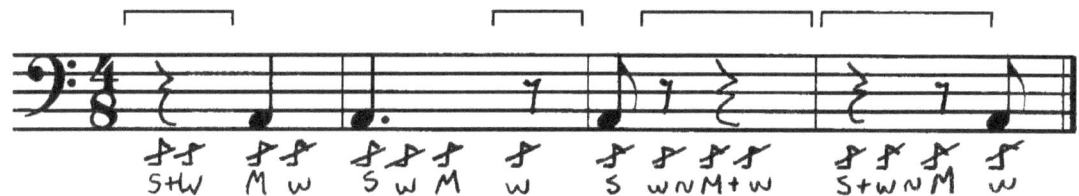

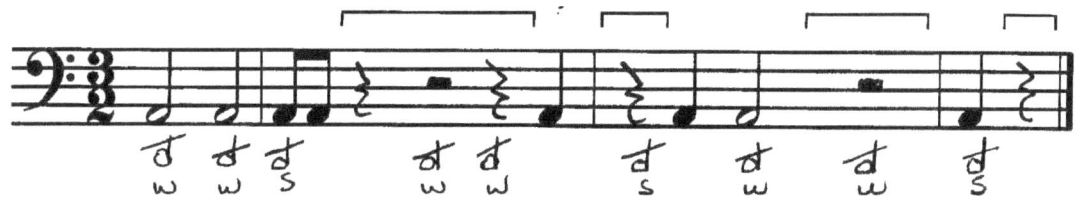

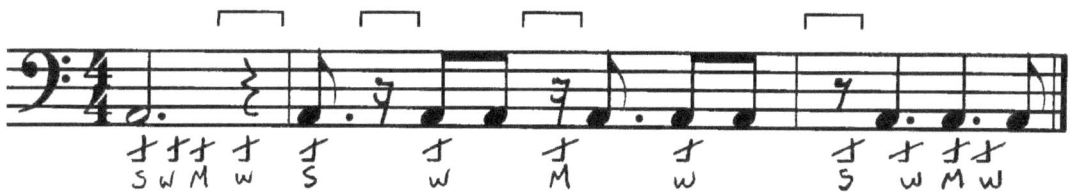

ULTIMATE MUSIC THEORY
BASIC EXAM SET #2 - EXAM #2

9. Match each musical sign or symbol with its English definition. (Not all definitions will be used.)

Sign or Symbol		Definition
		a) from the sign
p	f	b) becoming softer
<	h	c) hold for the combined value of the notes
𝄐	l	d) an octave
ff	g	e) pedal marking
♩♩ (tied)	c	f) soft
mf	k	g) very loud
♩	i	h) becoming louder
Ped.	e	i) detached
8va	d	j) play the notes *legato*
𝄋	a	k) moderately loud
		l) pause; hold the note ore rest longer than its written value

UltimateMusicTheory.com © Copyright 2013 Gloryland Publishing. All Rights Reserved.

ULTIMATE MUSIC THEORY
BASIC EXAM SET #2 - EXAM #2

10. Analyze the following excerpt by answering the questions below.

Minuet in G Major

W. F. Bach

[musical excerpt with markings A (Grazioso), B, C, D, E, F (triplet, 3), with circled notes labeled w.t. and s.t.]

a) Add the Time Signature directly on the music.

b) Name the key of this excerpt. __G Major__

c) Name the composer. __W. F. Bach__

d) Explain the term at A. __Grazioso - graceful__

e) The note at the letter **B** is the: ☐ Tonic ☒ Subdominant ☐ Dominant

f) The note at the letter **C** is the: ☐ Tonic ☐ Subdominant ☒ Dominant

g) Name the intervals at the letters: D __Maj 2__ E __Per 4__

h) Explain the sign at the letter F. __triplet - 3 notes played in the time of 2 notes of the same note value.__

i) Circle one example of a whole tone (whole step). Label it as **w.t.**

j) Circle one example of a semitone (half step). Label it as **s.t.**

UltimateMusicTheory.com © Copyright 2013 Gloryland Publishing. All Rights Reserved.

ULTIMATE MUSIC THEORY
BASIC EXAM SET #2 - EXAM #3

Total Score: ___/100

1. a) Write the following notes in the Treble Clef. Use whole notes.

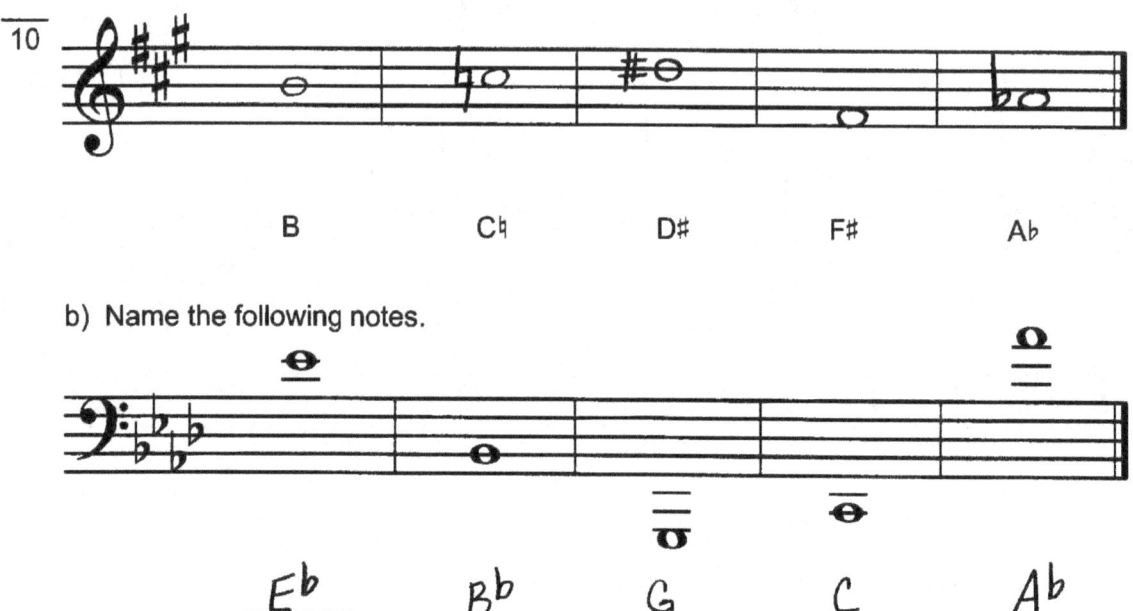

b) Name the following notes.

c) Write the following notes in the Bass Clef. Use whole notes.

d) Name the note below each bracket.

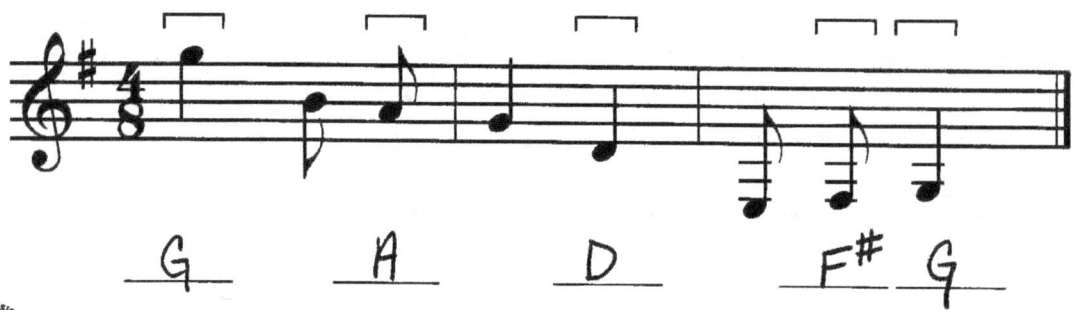

UltimateMusicTheory.com © Copyright 2013 Gloryland Publishing. All Rights Reserved.

ULTIMATE MUSIC THEORY
BASIC EXAM SET #2 - EXAM #3

2. a) Write the following solid triads in root position in the Treble Clef. Use the correct Key Signature and any necessary accidentals. Use whole notes.

Tonic triad of   Subdominant triad of   Dominant triad of
C Major   e minor harmonic   f sharp minor harmonic

b) Match each description in the left column with the correct triad in the right column.

Description	Answer		Triad
Tonic triad of F Major	d	a)	
Tonic triad of a minor harmonic	g	b)	
Subdominant triad of E Major	b	c)	
Dominant triad of d minor harmonic	a	d)	
Tonic triad of B flat Major	f	e)	
Subdominant triad of G Major	e	f)	
Dominant triad of E Major	c	g)	

UltimateMusicTheory.com © Copyright 2013 Gloryland Publishing. All Rights Reserved.

ULTIMATE MUSIC THEORY
BASIC EXAM SET #2 - EXAM #3

3. a) Name the following intervals.

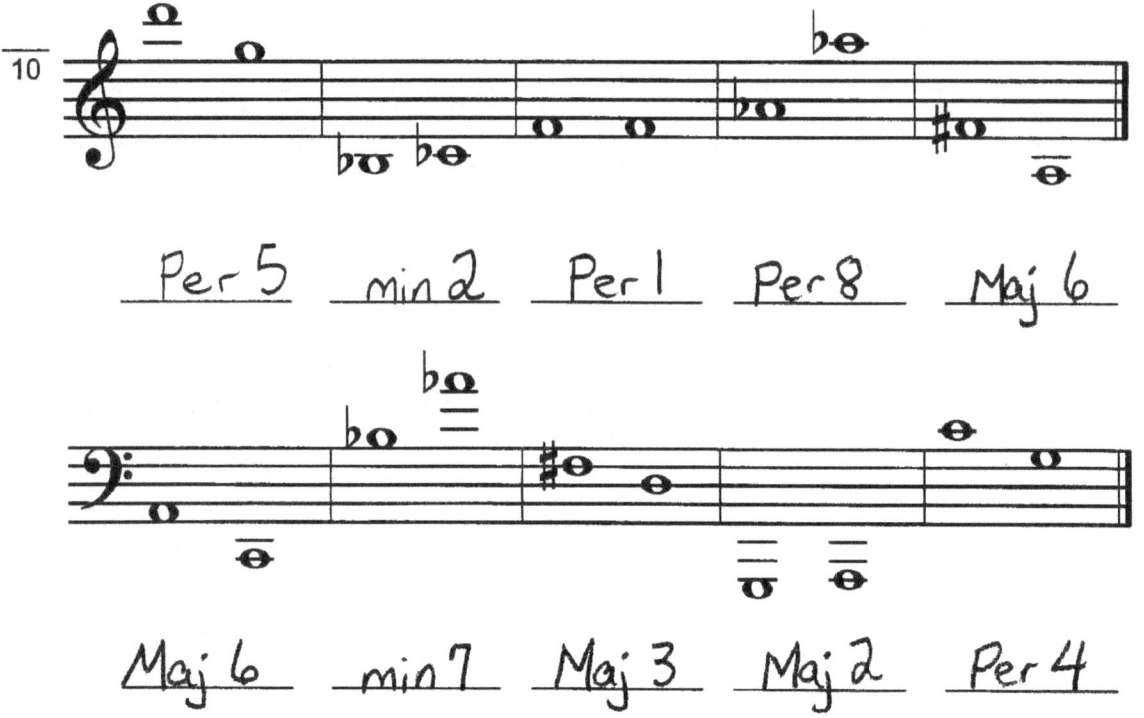

Per 5, min 2, Per 1, Per 8, Maj 6

Maj 6, min 7, Maj 3, Maj 2, Per 4

b) Write the harmonic interval above each of the given notes. Use whole notes.

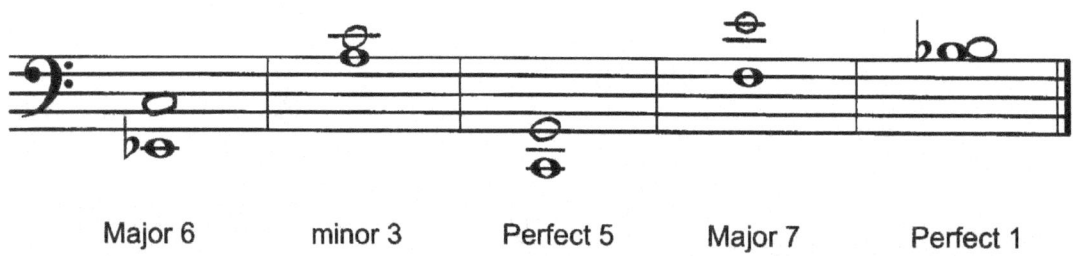

Major 6, minor 3, Perfect 5, Major 7, Perfect 1

c) Write the melodic interval above each of the given notes. Use half notes.

Major 3, minor 7, Perfect 4, minor 2, Perfect 8

UltimateMusicTheory.com © Copyright 2013 Gloryland Publishing. All Rights Reserved.

ULTIMATE MUSIC THEORY
BASIC EXAM SET #2 - EXAM #3

4. a) Name the key of the following melody. Rewrite the melody at the same pitch in the Bass Clef.

Key: b minor

b) Name the key of the following melody. Transpose it up one octave in the Treble Clef.

Key: A♭ Major

ULTIMATE MUSIC THEORY
BASIC EXAM SET #2 - EXAM #3

5. a) Write the g minor harmonic scale, ascending and descending, in the Bass Clef. Use a Key Signature and any necessary accidentals. Use whole notes.

b) Write the A flat Major scale, ascending and descending, in the Treble Clef. Use accidentals. Use whole notes.

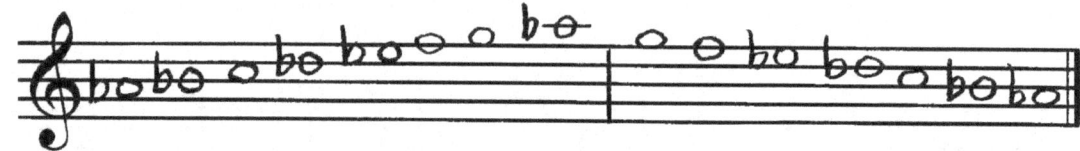

c) Write the c minor melodic scale, ascending and descending, in the Bass Clef. Use a Key Signature and any necessary accidentals. Use whole notes.

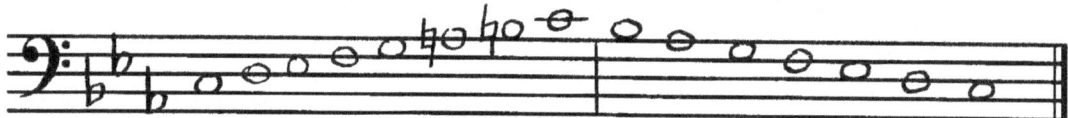

d) Write the D Major scale, ascending and descending, in the Treble Clef. Use a Key Signature. Use whole notes.

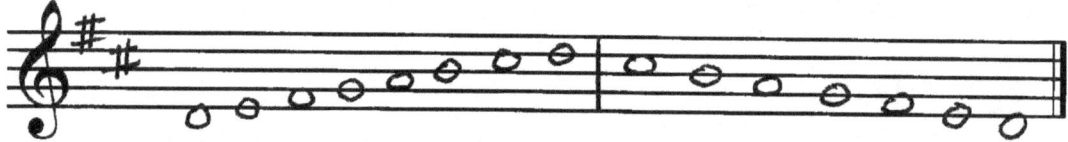

e) Write the e minor natural scale, ascending and descending, in the Bass Clef. Use accidentals. Use whole notes.

ULTIMATE MUSIC THEORY
BASIC EXAM SET #2 - EXAM #3

6. a) Name the Major key for each of the following Key Signatures.
    b) Name each of the given notes as: Tonic (T)
    Subdominant (SD)
    or Dominant (D)

a) A Major   B♭ Major   E♭ Major   E Major   A♭ Major
b)   D   SD   T   T   D

a) G Major   E Major   F Major   D Major   A♭ Major
b)   SD   SD   T   D   T

c) Name each of the following as: diatonic semitone or diatonic half step (**d.s.**)
                                 chromatic semitone or chromatic half step (**c.s.**)
                          whole tone or whole step (**w.t.**)
                    or enharmonic equivalent (**e.e.**)

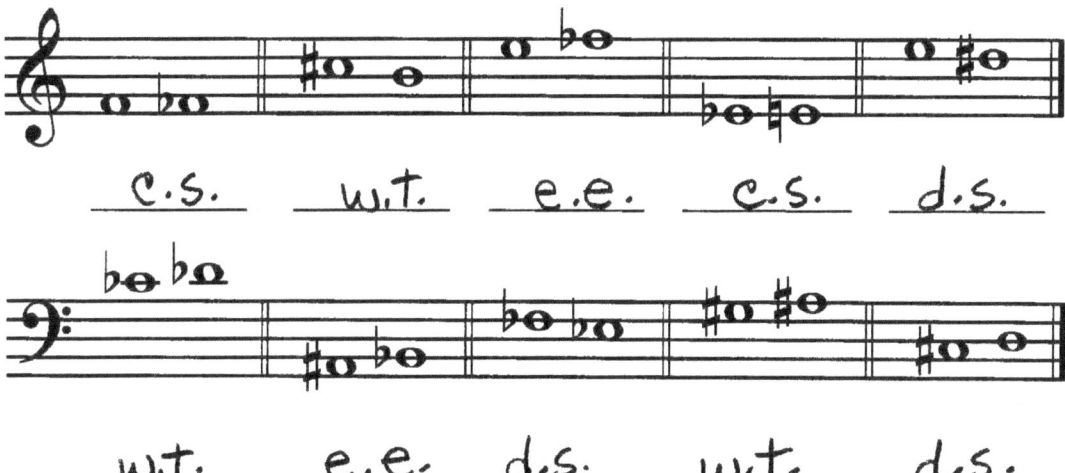

c.s.   w.t.   e.e.   c.s.   d.s.

w.t.   e.e.   d.s.   w.t.   d.s.

UltimateMusicTheory.com © Copyright 2013 Gloryland Publishing. All Rights Reserved.

ULTIMATE MUSIC THEORY
BASIC EXAM SET #2 - EXAM #3

7. a) Add bar lines to complete each of the following rhythms.

b) Add the correct Time Signature at the beginning of each of the following melodies.

ULTIMATE MUSIC THEORY
BASIC EXAM SET #2 - EXAM #3

8. Add rests below each bracket to complete each measure.

10

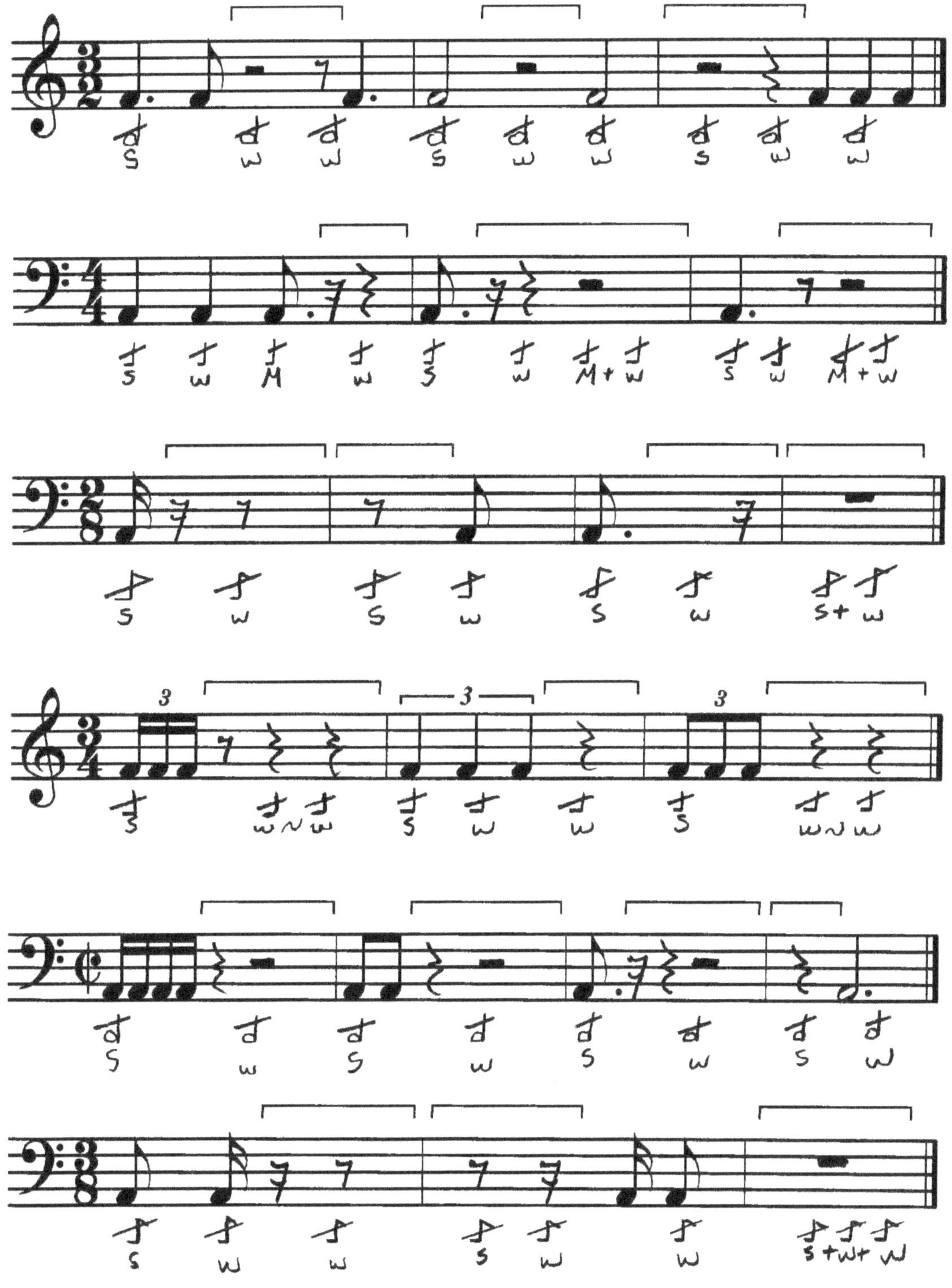

ULTIMATE MUSIC THEORY
BASIC EXAM SET #2 - EXAM #3

9. For each of the following Italian terms, circle TRUE if the definition is true (correct) or circle FALSE if the definition is false (incorrect).

___
10

	True or False	Italian Term	Definition
Example:	TRUE or (FALSE)	fortissimo	soft
a)	TRUE or (FALSE)	presto	as fast as possible
b)	(TRUE) or FALSE	largo	very slow
c)	(TRUE) or FALSE	con pedale	with pedal
d)	TRUE or (FALSE)	crescendo	gradually slower
e)	TRUE or (FALSE)	allegretto	very fast
f)	(TRUE) or FALSE	grazioso	graceful
g)	(TRUE) or FALSE	forte	loud
h)	(TRUE) or FALSE	mano sinistra, M.S.	left hand
i)	TRUE or (FALSE)	andantino	moderately slow, at a walking pace
j)	TRUE or (FALSE)	dal segno, D.S.	repeat from the beginning and end at *Fine*

ULTIMATE MUSIC THEORY
BASIC EXAM SET #2 - EXAM #3

10. Analyze the following excerpt by answering the questions below.

Fantasia
G. P. Telemann
(1681 - 1767)

a) Explain the Time Signature. _Cut time is 2/2 time_

b) Name the key of this excerpt. _C Major_

c) Name the Composer. _G.P. Telemann_

d) In what year was the Composer born? _1681_

e) How many measures are in this excerpt? _4_

f) How many slurs are in this excerpt? _3_

g) Name the intervals at the letters: A _Per 5_ B _min 6_

h) Circle an example of a diatonic semitone (diatonic half step). Label it **d.s.**

i) The note at the letter **C** is the: ☐ Tonic ☒ Subdominant ☐ Dominant

j) The note at the letter **D** is the: ☐ Tonic ☐ Subdominant ☒ Dominant

UltimateMusicTheory.com © Copyright 2013 Gloryland Publishing. All Rights Reserved.

ULTIMATE MUSIC THEORY
BASIC EXAM SET #2 – EXAM #4

Total Score: ___/100

1. a) Write the following notes on ledger lines either above or below the Treble Clef. Use half notes.

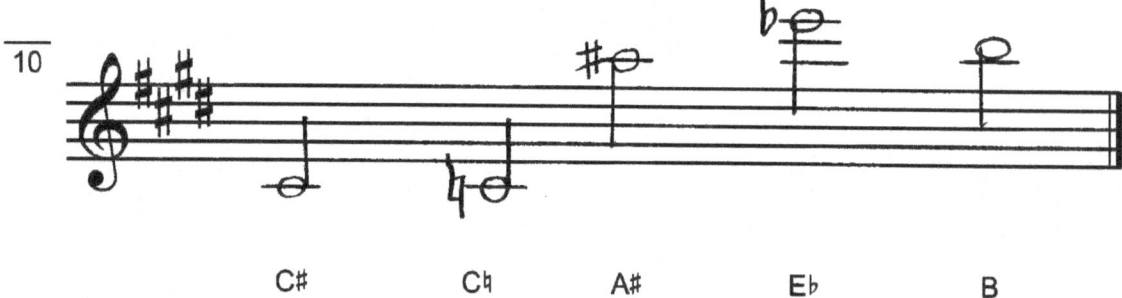

C#   C♮   A#   E♭   B

b) In the measure beside each note, write its enharmonic equivalent. Use whole notes. Name both notes.

B♭   A#   F   E#   B#   C

G♭   F#   D#   E♭   E   F♭

c) Name the following notes.

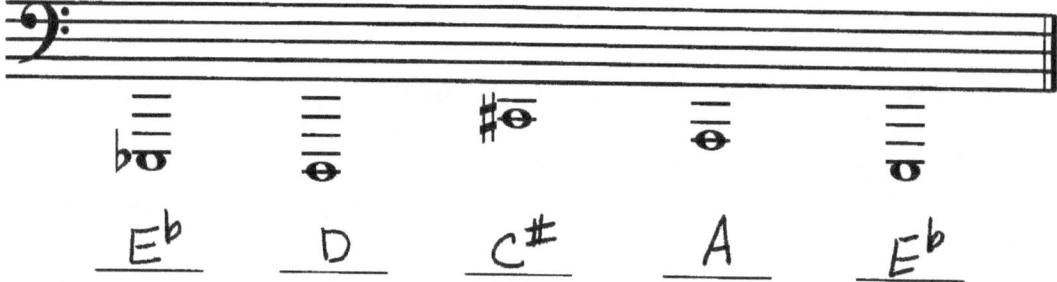

E♭   D   C#   A   E♭

UltimateMusicTheory.com © Copyright 2013 Gloryland Publishing. All Rights Reserved.

ULTIMATE MUSIC THEORY
BASIC EXAM SET #2 - EXAM #4

2. a) Write the following notes in the Treble Clef. Use accidentals. Use whole notes.

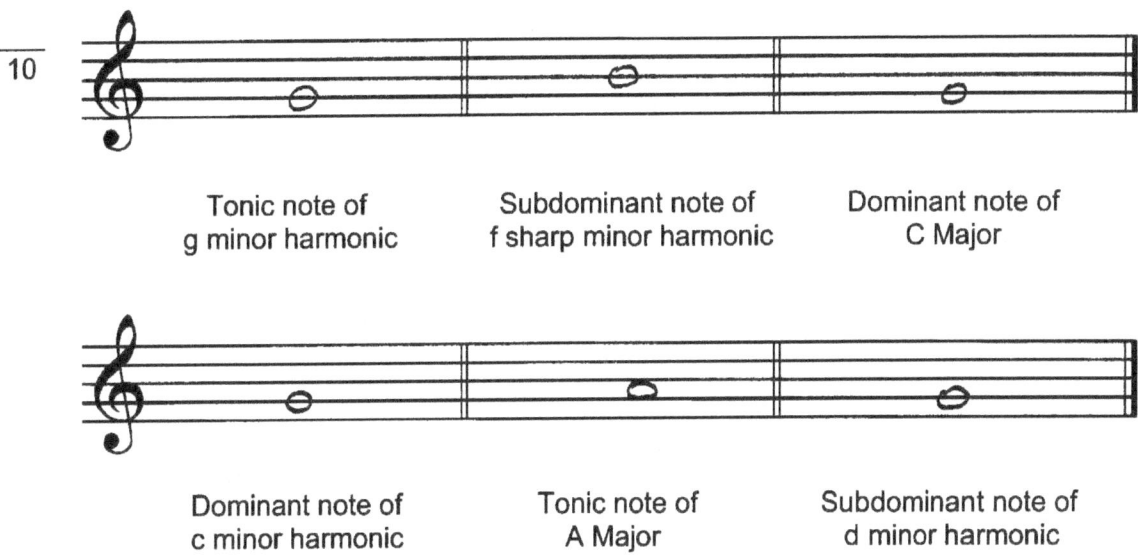

| Tonic note of | Subdominant note of | Dominant note of |
| g minor harmonic | f sharp minor harmonic | C Major |

| Dominant note of | Tonic note of | Subdominant note of |
| c minor harmonic | A Major | d minor harmonic |

b) Write the following solid (blocked) triads in root position in the Bass Clef. Use a Key Signature and any necessary accidentals. Use whole notes.

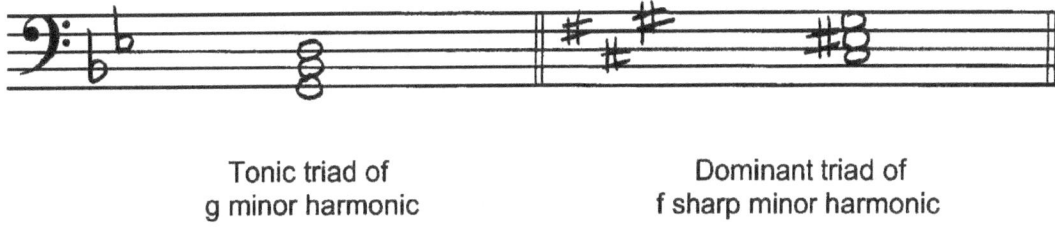

Tonic triad of g minor harmonic   Dominant triad of f sharp minor harmonic

Dominant triad of E flat Major   Subdominant triad of D Major

ULTIMATE MUSIC THEORY
BASIC EXAM SET #2 - EXAM #4

3. a) Name the following intervals.

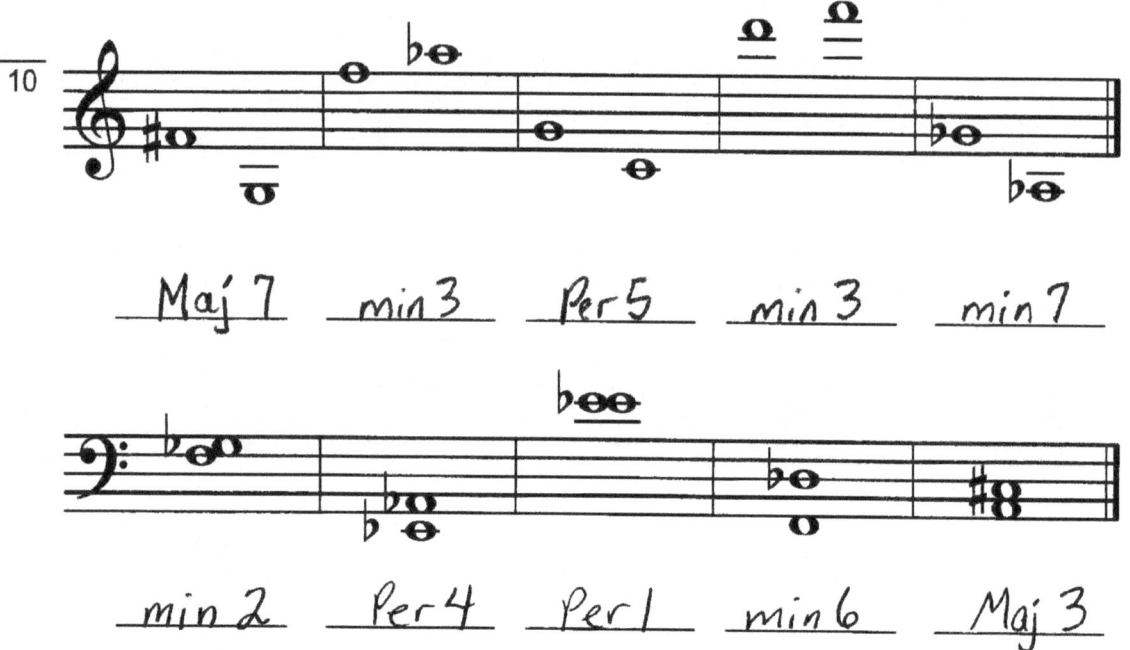

b) Write the harmonic interval above each of the given notes. Use whole notes.

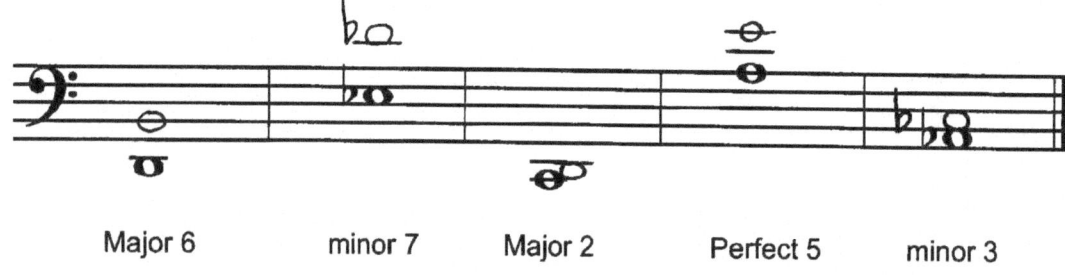

c) Write the melodic interval above each of the given notes. Use half notes.

ULTIMATE MUSIC THEORY
BASIC EXAM SET #2 - EXAM #4

4. a) Name the key of the following melody. Rewrite the melody at the same pitch in the Treble Clef.

Key: e minor

b) Name the key of the following melody. Transpose it down one octave in the Bass Clef.

Key: D Major

ULTIMATE MUSIC THEORY
BASIC EXAM SET #2 - EXAM #4

5. a) Write the d minor harmonic scale, ascending and descending, in the Bass Clef. Use a Key Signature and any necessary accidentals. Use whole notes.

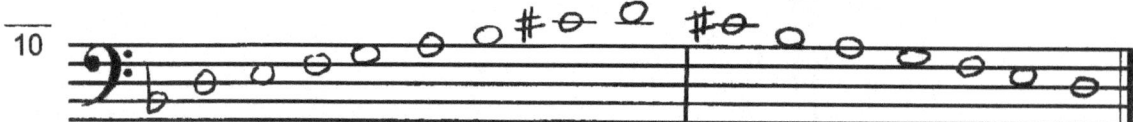

b) Write the B flat Major scale, ascending and descending, in the Treble Clef. Use accidentals. Use whole notes.

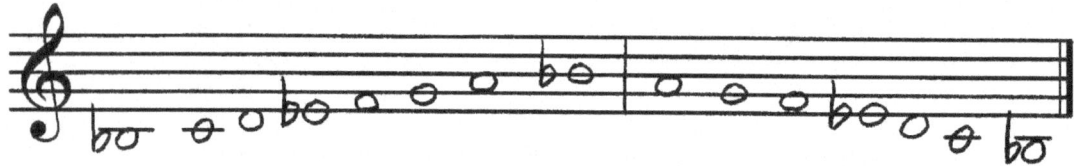

c) Write the f sharp minor natural scale, ascending and descending, in the Bass Clef. Use accidentals. Use whole notes.

d) Write the A Major scale, ascending and descending, in the Treble Clef. Use a Key Signature. Use whole notes.

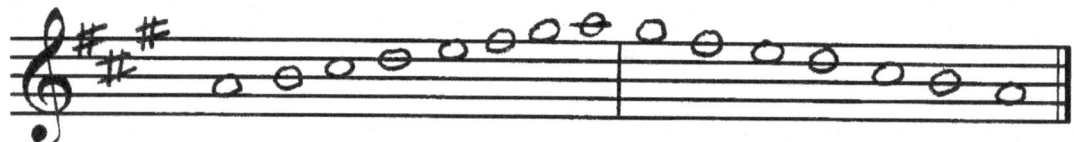

e) Identify the Major Key for each of the following Key Signatures.

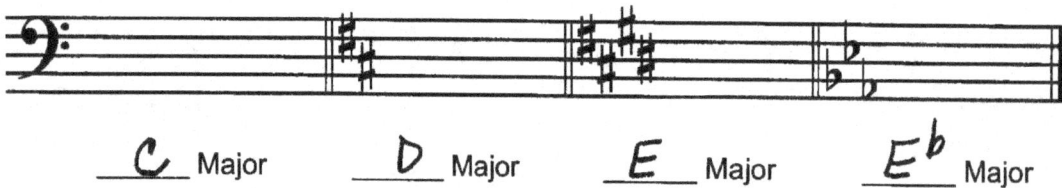

__C__ Major   __D__ Major   __E__ Major   __E♭__ Major

ULTIMATE MUSIC THEORY
BASIC EXAM SET #2 - EXAM #4

6. a) Name the minor key for each of the following Key Signatures.
    b) Name each of the given notes as: Tonic (**T**)
    Subdominant (**SD**)
    or Dominant (**D**)

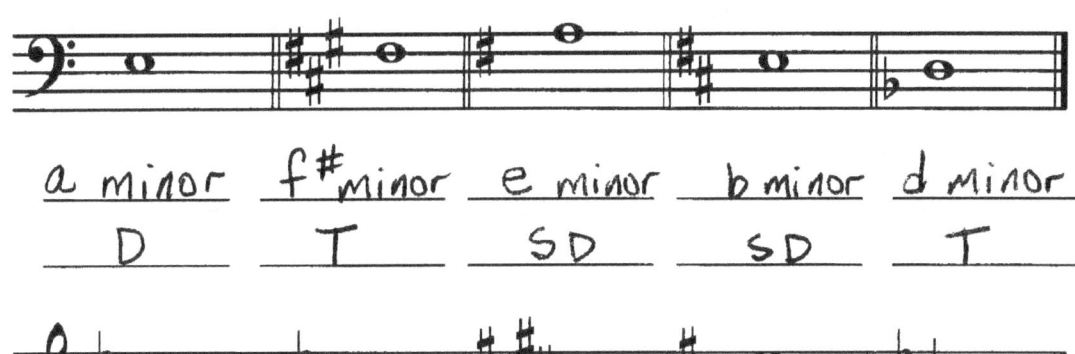

a) a minor | f# minor | e minor | b minor | d minor
b) D | T | SD | SD | T

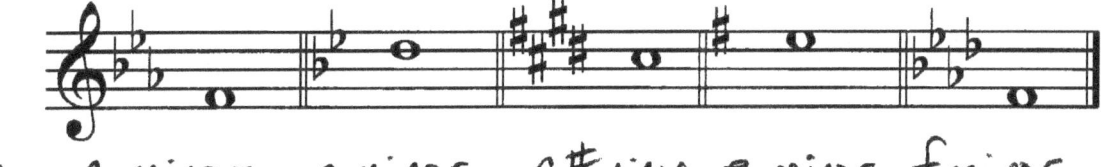

a) c minor | g minor | c# minor | e minor | f minor
b) SD | D | T | T | T

c) Name each of the following as: diatonic semitone or diatonic half step (**d.s.**)
    chromatic semitone or chromatic half step (**c.s.**)
    whole tone or whole step (**w.t.**)
    or enharmonic equivalent (**e.e.**)

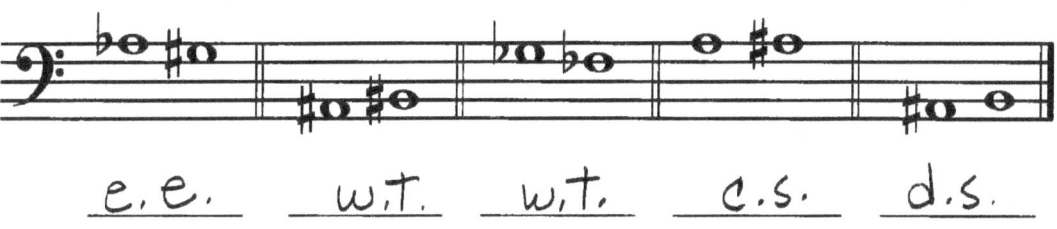

e.e. | w.t. | w.t. | c.s. | d.s.

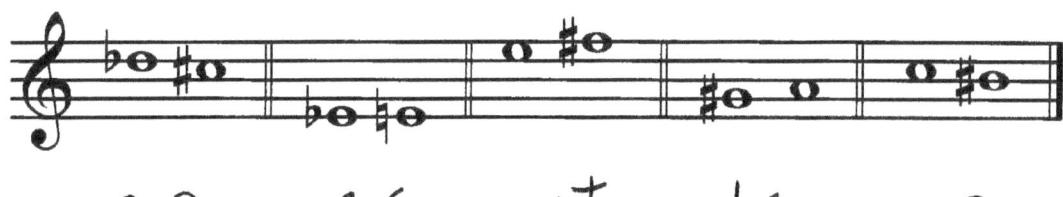

e.e. | c.s. | w.t | d.s. | e.e.

ULTIMATE MUSIC THEORY
BASIC EXAM SET #2 - EXAM #4

7. a) Add bar lines to complete each of the following rhythms.

b) Add the correct Time Signature at the beginning of the following melodies.

ULTIMATE MUSIC THEORY
BASIC EXAM SET #2 - EXAM #4

8. Add rests below each bracket to complete each measure.

ULTIMATE MUSIC THEORY
BASIC EXAM SET #2 - EXAM #4

9. Match each musical term with its symbol or sign. (Not all symbols or signs will be used.)

Term — **Symbol or Sign**

a) 𝅗𝅥 (with accent)

pianissimo — c   b) ⌞___⌟

mezzo piano — g   c) **pp**

forte — l   d) <

accent — a   e) 8va- - - ⌐

decrescendo — i   f) 8va- - - ⌟

slur — k   g) *mp*

octave below — f   h) ♩ ♩

pedal marking — b   i) >

octave above — e   j) 𝄆 𝄇

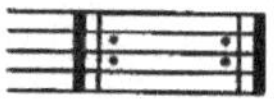

repeat sign — j   k) ♩ ♩ ♩

                       l) *f*

ULTIMATE MUSIC THEORY
BASIC EXAM SET #2 - EXAM #4

10. Analyze the following piece of music by answering the questions below.

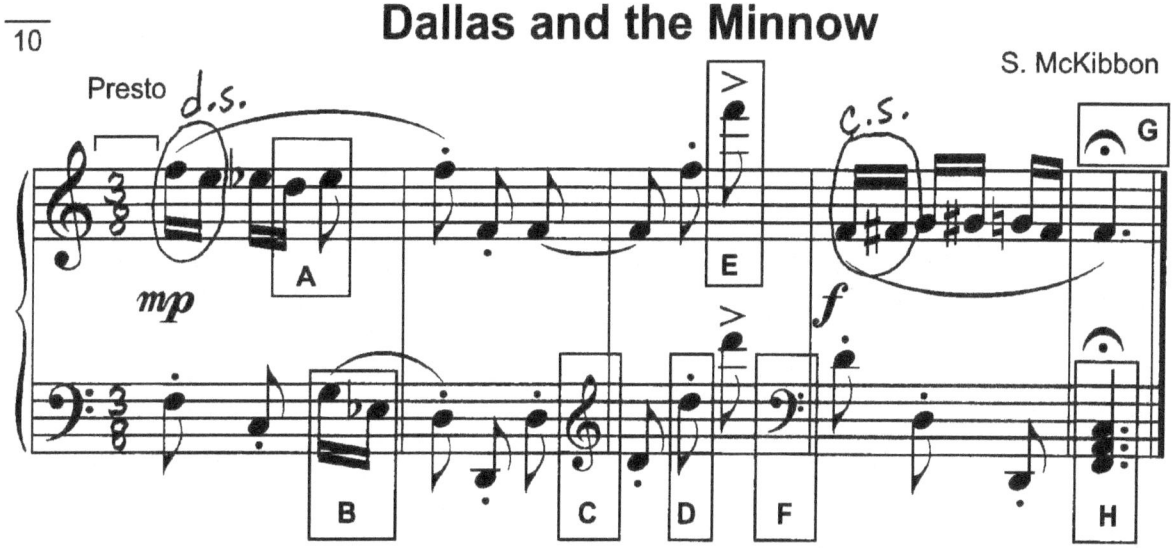

a) Add the Time Signature directly on the music.

b) Name the intervals at the letters: A _min 2_   B _Maj 3_

c) Explain the sign at the letter C. _left hand will play in the Treble Clef_

d) Name the notes at the letters: D _D_   E _F_

e) Explain the sign at the letter F. _left hand will play in the Bass Clef_

f) Explain the sign at the letter G. _fermata - pause, hold longer than the written value_

g) How many slurs are there in this piece? _three_

h) The triad at the letter H is: ☐ d minor   ☒ F Major   ☐ f minor

i) Circle one example of a chromatic semitone (half step). Label it as **c.s.**

j) Circle one example of a diatonic semitone (half step). Label it as **d.s.**

UltimateMusicTheory.com © Copyright 2013 Gloryland Publishing. All Rights Reserved.

 **Workbooks, Exams, Answers, Online Courses, App & More!**

A Proven Step-by-Step System to Learn Theory Faster - from Beginner to Advanced.

Innovative techniques designed to develop a complete understanding of music theory, to enhance sight reading, ear training, creativity, composition and musical expression.

All UMT Series have matching Answer Books!

The UMT Rudiments Series - Beginner A, Beginner B, Beginner C, Prep 1, Prep 2, Basic, Intermediate, Advanced & Complete (All-In-One)

- ♪ 12 Lessons, Review Tests, and a Final Exam to develop confidence
- ♪ Music Theory Guide & Chart for fast and easy reference of theory concepts
- ♪ 80 Flashcards for fun drills to dramatically increase retention & comprehension

Rudiments Exam Series - Preparatory, Basic, Intermediate & Advanced

- ♪ 8 Exams plus UMT Tips on How to Score 100% on Theory Exams

Each Rudiments Workbook correlates to a Supplemental Workbook.

The UMT Supplemental Series - Prep Level, Level 1, Level 2, Level 3, Level 4, Level 5, Level 6, Level 7, Level 8 & Complete (All-In-One) Level

- ♪ Form & Analysis and Music History - Composers, Eras & Musical Styles
- ♪ Melody Writing using ICE - Imagine, Compose & Explore
- ♪ 12 Lessons, Review Tests, Final Exam and 80 Flashcards for quick study

Supplemental Exam Series - Level 5, Level 6, Level 7 & Level 8

- ♪ 8 Exams to successfully prepare for nationally recognized Theory Exams

UMT Online Courses, Music Theory App & More

- ♪ UMT Certification Course, Teachers Membership & Elite Educator Program
- ♪ Ultimate Music Theory App correlates to the Rudiments Workbooks
- ♪ Free Resources - Teachers Guide, Music Theory Blogs, videos & downloads

Go To: **UltimateMusicTheory.com**

www.ingramcontent.com/pod-product-compliance
Lightning Source LLC
Chambersburg PA
CBHW081735100526
44591CB00016B/2624